# WELSHPOOL & LLANFAIR LIGHT RAILWAY THROUGH THE YEARS

## by Oliver Edwards

Published by Mainline & Maritime Ltd, 3 Broadleaze, Upper Seagry, near Chippenham, SN15 5EY
Tel: 01275 845012
www.mainlineandmaritime.co.uk        orders@mainlineandmaritime.co.uk
Printed in the UK

ISBN: 978-1-900340-63-2    © Mainline & Maritime Ltd, Oliver Edwards & Photographers 2020

**Front Cover** A timeless W&L scene - a mixed train featuring 823 THE COUNTESS and the three 'Pickerings', all in GWR livery.

*Keith Halton*

**Back Cover** The archetypal 'preservation era' W&L - 822 THE EARL heads a rake of imported carriages at Castle Caereinion.

*Anthony Haynes*

**Above** Seen crossing the Banwy Bridge, visiting locomotive ZILLERTAL is framed by the trees which line the river. It is heading towards Llanfair with a busy train in the autumn of 2019. The arrival of the locomotive caused sustained enthusiast interest throughout this period, with phones ringing 'off the hook' to enquire after its next operating day.

*Anthony Haynes*

# INTRODUCTION

Readers,

Thank you very much for purchasing this album of Welshpool & Llanfair Light Railway photographs through the ages. It will give you a brief look at the working life of the railway before reflecting on some of the developments of the line in preservation including locomotive arrivals and departures and special events. It is not intended as a definitive history of the railway, but should be a great introduction to our line for those who are unfamiliar with it and as a great reminder for others. Many of the images in this book have been rarely seen in public before, surprising even some seasoned volunteers!

This book has been produced as one part of the W&L's Tracks to Recovery appeal, with a huge thank you necessary to Iain McCall of Mainline and Maritime for his invaluable assistance. Tracks to Recovery was launched as a way to counteract the negative effects of our closure because of the impacts of COVID-19 restrictions. It is not clear at the time of writing how long the closure will last but already several key weeks of revenue have been lost and many more may have also been consigned to the scrapheap by the end of this period in world history. Your purchase has helped us to maintain our reserves, despite still having substantial costs to meet, and we are grateful for it.

It would be remiss not to thank all those photographers who have contributed to the production of this book through the use of their images. They have been a critical resource in our Tracks to Recovery appeal and have brought a great amount of pleasure to all those who have accessed their images, either through Facebook or in this publication. It has not always been possible to recognise the photographer on some of our archive images, but we are as undoubtedly grateful for their efforts as those of any other.

Thank you, and enjoy

*Oliver Edwards - Author / Compiler.*

# A BRIEF HISTORY OF THE LINE

As one of the last common carrier narrow gauge railways to be constructed in Britain, the Welshpool & Llanfair Light Railway has always held a special place in the hearts of Mid Wales residents and railway enthusiasts alike. Today, it can, totally authentically, recreate trains from the 1920s and the 1950s on the line as well as scenes from as far away as Austria and Sierra Leone. At eight miles, it is one of the longer narrow gauge preserved lines in Wales and is proud to be a 'Great Little Train' of this country despite being only a dozen or so miles from the English border. This brief section outlines the history of the line.

Construction of the W&L began in 1901, following many years of local interest in improving what would today be known as the connectivity of the town of Llanfair Caereinion and the villages and hamlets between it and Welshpool. Funded by local subscription, significant investment by the Earl of Powis - a local dignitary - and the support of local authorities (which in itself was a novelty), the W&L was built as a light railway under the Light Railways Act of 1896. This legislation allowed for cheaper construction, avoiding some of the stringent measures imposed on mainline railway companies to encourage lines that were expected to be fairly unremunerative for shareholders. The line was built by a specially formed company who then leased the line to the Cambrian Railways who, whilst a small name nationally, had a considerable network in the region.

Opened on April 4th 1903, the railway included a town section of street running between the mainline station and Raven Square where the current line is picked up to head to Llanfair. From that day, the line settled into a calm and humble existence transporting freight in the form of farm produce and livestock and coal, among other supplies, and moving passengers, who particularly used the line on Welshpool market days. The W&L differs from many narrow gauge Welsh railways in that it never carried slate or tourists. Instead, it relied on agricultural traffic and this made it unusual.

When the railways were grouped into four large companies in the early 1920s, the W&L joined the rest of the Cambrian network as part of the Great Western. The W&L is, unlike some narrow gauge railways, the servant of communities relatively easily accessed by road, even in the last century. This meant the Great Western found it easy to introduce bus services to compete with its own trains, eventually causing the termination of passenger services in 1931. Whereas some routes, such as the Leek and Manifold and Glyn Valley Tramway, closed during this period, the W&L still had a reasonable traffic in freight and it operated goods trains through World War Two and beyond nationalisation in 1948. By 1956, though, the line was designated for closure and it shut following the operation of an enthusiast special on the 3rd November that year.

This may have been the end of the story, as it was for so many others, but for the determination of preservationists. By fundraising and negotiation with British Railways, this small band of volunteers could begin work on the line in 1959 before securing a lease in 1962. Whereas the earlier preserved railways like the Talyllyn had been taken over from private companies, the W&L was the first former British Railways line where such discussions took place, helping to pave the way for groups around the UK. Reopened between Castle Caereinion and Llanfair in April 1963, the 'modern' W&L has been rebuilt by the sweat, love and donations of a 'railway family' ever since. Important moments are highlighted through this book, but they include reopening the line to Welshpool in 1981 and the arrival of replica Pickering carriages from 2004.

The W&L today operates for eight miles between Llanfair and Welshpool. It passes through halts at Heniarth, Cyfronydd, Castle Caereinion and Sylfaen on the way, each of which served farms or, in the case of Castle Caereinion, a small village. The railway's 'light' nature meant it avoided heavy engineering such as cuttings or tunnels where possible, creating a railway which frequently tackles relatively short but in places seriously steep gradients. The exception to this rule is the Golfa bank, a lengthy stretch of 1 in 29 gradient that comes immediately after departing Welshpool station. One of the special features of W&L services is that passengers are allowed to ride on the balconies of the carriages, giving them unrivalled views of the picturesque scenery surround the railway and of the locomotive hauling their train at work.

Today, W&L services run for approximately 150 days per year, excluding the Santa train season in December. You can find details of train times and operating dates, as well as how to become a member and special events, at www.wllr.org.uk.

**Left** Having left the Banwy Bridge with a four carriage train, THE EARL drifts on towards Llanfair. The line climbs between Heniarth, the halt the train will pass through momentarily, and Llanfair, although on nothing like the severity of gradient seen following THE EARL's departure from Welshpool. This section, with the river alongside for most of the remaining journey, provides views of the wildlife surrounding the railway which are not possible from the road.

*Anthony Haynes*

This photograph, showing the W&L before 1923, shows the W&L as the country byway it was throughout its life. We see a mixed train, corrugated station office and a surprisingly large team of seven railway employees.

*W&L Archives*

The W&L is famed in railway circles for its former town section, bringing its narrow gauge tracks through the heart of the market town of Welshpool to meet the mainline exchange sidings. Now gone, with little reason and great difficulty involved in any reinstatement effort, the town section is beautifully remembered in this image of a freight bound for the mainline crossing Church Street.

*W&L Archives*

Seen departing Welshpool on a mixed train, which were very typical on the W&L up to the loss of passenger services in 1931, is a 'Beyer' before rebuilding but post-grouping in 1923. The lack of transferring passengers between the mainline and W&L services is apparent here, with plenty of room in the train's two Pickering carriages!

*W&L Archives*

The two locomotives of the W&L were 'westernised' in 1929-30 when they were rebuilt with re-designed boilers and standard GW fittings. The engines were not taken to Swindon for this work. Instead, this work was carried out in Oswestry, where the new boilers were delivered. This image shows THE COUNTESS, with shortened nameplates in their new cabside position, in Welshpool at some time between 1923 and 1930, in GW livery but with original chimney and boiler.

*W&L Archives*

This undated view of both THE EARL and THE COUNTESS in Welshpool shows the locomotive stabling facilities of the railway during its working life. Today, facilities are concentrated at the Llanfair end of the line, where preservation efforts began in the 1960s.

*W&L Archives*

Freight was transhipped at the Welshpool exchange sidings with the former Cambrian Railways mainline. Initial proposals around the time of the railway's inception foresaw the use of transporter wagons, on which standard gauge wagons could be moved along the W&L, though these were never adopted.

*W&L Archives*

The Boy and The Earl. In September 1956, THE EARL heads along the town section of the W&L, weaving through the parked cars and houses that dot the route and admired by an intrigued young boy.

*Douglas Robinson*

Heading through the streets of Welshpool, THE EARL, by this stage unnamed, heads a goods train. Already, we can see a number of cars in the archive element of this image, demonstrating the decline of the railways generally in favour of the private car. Today, you can follow the route of the W&L's former town section on an informative town trail with artwork and interpretation.

*Douglas Robinson*

Railways such as the W&L were transformative investments in the regions that they served, though they were infamously light on traffic revenues. The W&L, though it lost its passenger service in 1931, did carry reasonable amounts of freight. This image shows a train in Llanfair in September 1956 with no less than eight wagons in view.

*Douglas Robinson*

By now in the last throes of its working life, the W&L's middle station, Castle Caereinion, is seen here in September 1956. THE EARL heads a Welshpool-bound train through the rundown station. It is worth crediting the enginemen of the line for the state of cleanliness in which the locomotives were kept, even in this last operating year. Of note in this image is the rusting 1919-built Burrell traction engine which had worked on local farms before being laid up. This is now, happily, preserved.

*Douglas Robinson*

The W&L was closed in a spectacular and very public way with the Stephenson Locomotive Society special on the line on the 3rd of November 1956. Enthusiasts rode in the open wagons of the train. The special stands here, on the return journey to Welshpool, at the water tower just outside Llanfair.

*W&L Archives*

Following withdrawal, THE EARL and THE COUNTESS were stored at the former Cambrian Railways works at Oswestry, kept safe from the once seemingly inevitable scrapman's torch, while early preservationists negotiated with British Railways.

*Alan Lewis Chambers*

Tentative line clearance had begun in 1959, moving on to the forming of a preservation company in 1960 and the signing of a lease in 1962. This scene shows THE EARL shunting at Llanfair in August 1961, just weeks after having been returned to the line, in a striking grey undercoat. Volunteers of this period relate that at least one cyclist was knocked off course by the sight of this 'ghost train'.

*Ron Fisher*

Before the reopening of most lines as heritage railways, some civil engineering inspection and shrub clearance is generally needed. Now painted in plain black but with Cambrian nameplate positioning and polished safety valve cover, THE EARL stands in Castle Caereinion loop with a works train in March 1962.

*Ron Fisher*

The closure of the Upnor and Lodge Hill Railway, a military railway in Kent, brought the opportunity to purchase rolling stock for the enthusiastic members who had taken over the W&L. This was particularly welcome as the company had no passenger rolling stock until the arrival of four passenger carriages from the U&LHR, some of which are preparing to be unloaded here at Welshpool, in front of Boys and Boden hardware supplies who still trade today.

*W&L Archives*

After the arrival of the preservation company, running on the town section continued for some time, primarily to fetch rolling stock from the exchange sidings from the mainline between Shrewsbury and Machynlleth. Here, THE COUNTESS, making an impressive demonstration of her abilities, leads THE EARL with a train of newly arrived wagons from the Upnor & Lodge Hill Railway.

*W&L Archives*

Coaling up ahead of the reopening train on the 6th April 1963, THE EARL stands in the yard at Llanfair. Both THE EARL and THE COUNTESS took part in this special occasion.

*Ray Hulock*

THE COUNTESS shunts the coaches for the reopening train here. Though services only ran as far as Castle Caereinion in the timetable of the newly formed company, opening day services ran as far as the exchange sidings at Welshpool and, judging by Press Association footage of the day, caused great local interest.

*Ray Hulock*

Seen here in July 1963, just three months after the reopening of the railway, is a typical W&L train of the period. Headed by THE EARL, the train includes four vehicles. Notably, these early trains included a W&L brake van and the 'Combination Car' at the end of the train. This coach was another former Upnor resident and featured several compartments for military officers. It is now used on the Welsh Highland Railway.

*Ron Fisher*

This time seen at Castle Caereinion, an early train is surrounded by a reasonable crowd of passengers, suggesting the early abilities of the preservationists to attract attention to their efforts. This is further substantiated by the several Movietone and Press Association films of the restoration of the railway through the 1960s.

*Dennis John Norton*

One noticeable feature of this period was the smartly turned out rolling stock. Initially painted in a vivid green, the former Upnor & Lodge Hill Railway carriages were gradually rebuilt during this period with windows and doors before being sold to the Sittingbourne and Kemsley Light Railway.

*W&L Archives*

The early efforts of the preservationists at Welshpool were very nearly dashed after flooding caused serious damage, the impact of which can be seen in this image, to the Banwy Bridge in 1964. This structure carries the railway over the Banwy river just after Heniarth, a farm halt on the line (when travelling in the Welshpool direction). Without the bridge, the W&L would have been destined to become a much shorter railway and may not have survived in this truncated fashion. Fortunately, the 16th Railway Regiment Royal Engineers were convinced to help restore the structure and it was completed in August 1965. A relief indeed!

*W&L Archives*

Dignity & Impudence - The two original locomotives of the W&L, THE EARL and THE COUNTESS, were built in 1902 by Beyer, Peacock & Co Ltd in Manchester ahead of the opening of the line in 1903. In this image, we see THE EARL stood with 1458, an ex-Great Western 14xx 0-4-2T on the 16th July 1963. It has been widely suggested that 1458 was sent to Welshpool specifically to pose for the photograph.

*W&L Archives*

In more recent times, THE EARL has been turned out in simple, unlined black which contrasts well with the more elegant Great Western green of THE COUNTESS. Here, THE EARL arrives at Llanfair on a typical, 1990s/2000s W&L train.

*Andrew Simmonds*

THE COUNTESS was turned out in a lined version of the former Cambrian Railways livery in its first period of preserved operation. Here, likely on the same trip as we saw earlier bringing new rolling stock from Upnor, THE COUNTESS leads THE EARL through Castle Caereinion.

*W&L Archives*

THE EARL and THE COUNTESS were named in tribute to the Earl and Countess of Powis, who supported the railway's construction. The modern Earl of Powis is now the President of the W&L. THE COUNTESS - locomotive, not lady - shunts here during the 2013 gala at Welshpool.

*Andrew Simmonds*

In searching for additional steam motive power for the W&L, preservationists found No. 85 in Sierra Leone. Built in 1954 for the Sierra Leone Government Railway, it arrives here in Llanfair in a seemingly careworn state. Looks, though, can deceive and the locomotive was steamed just three days after arrival, on August 10th 1975.

*Bruce Webber*

Popular with crews and generally well-loved at the W&L, No. 85 has carried a great range of liveries during its operations in Mid Wales. Here, it appears in lined madder lake, though it has also worked in apple green, midnight blue and black. Notably, here it is paired with a former Sierra Leone Railways carriage.

*Andrew Simmonds*

No. 85 remains one of the smaller 'core pool' locomotives in the W&L fleet. As at other railways, locomotives in service, restoration and storage are rotated between these states. No. 85 is currently displayed awaiting restoration. It is seen here during the final days of its last boiler ticket at Welshpool water tower.

*Andrew Simmonds*

JOAN, a Stoke-on-Trent built 0-6-2 tank, is pictured in a familiar bright blue livery in Llanfair station yard. A product of Kerr, Stuart & Co Ltd, JOAN was exported in 1927 to operate sugar cane railways in Antigua in the West Indies. It has operated two stints at the W&L, from 1977 to 1991 and 2011 until withdrawal in late 2019.

*Andrew Simmonds*

DOUGAL, No.8 in the W&L's numbering scheme, is the smallest steam locomotive at the railway. It was built by Andrew Barclay, Sons & Co Ltd in 1946 to work the restrictively gauged railways of Provan Gasworks in Glasgow. This image shows the locomotive in the early days of preservation at the W&L, when it carried an arresting shade of red.

*W&L Archives*

Once retired in 1961, DOUGAL was rescued by the Railway Enthusiasts Club who moved it to Farnborough in Hampshire. It was then purchased by Ralph Russell, who brought it to the W&L for restoration. This photograph, from several years later, shows the locomotive in an attractive darker green than today.

*Andrew Simmonds*

DOUGAL is now fitted with a larger set of tanks which has improved the locomotive's water capacity, though it remains too small for regular trains. Here, it runs off the Banwy Bridge towards Cyfronydd, during the 2006 Gala Weekend.

*David Marsh*

The W&L has gained a reputation as the home of many international artefacts over the last 60 years and No. 699.01 is a particularly interesting one. Built as a tender engine for the German Military Railways in 1944 in occupied France, its working life was largely spent in Austria on scenic lines such as from Weiz to Ratten. For this route, it was rebuilt as a tank engine, creating a well-proportioned locomotive. Now carrying the name SIR DREFALDWYN, which is Welsh for County of Montgomery, it can manage similar train weights to THE EARL and THE COUNTESS.

*Andrew Simmonds*

MONARCH is, perhaps, the most unusual locomotive based at the W&L. Built by W. G. Bagnall in 1953 using the concept of two articulated bogies, which is very popular abroad but was never widely adopted in the UK, MONARCH entered traffic that year on the Bowaters Paper Mill system at Sittingbourne. The engine was particularly useful on the W&L in the hot summer of 1976, when it was used extensively and 'clocked up' 1948 miles. It was sold later for an abortive project at the Ffestiniog Railway and was returned to the W&L for cosmetic restoration and display at Welshpool.

*Alan Doig*

David and Goliath, or is it DOUGAL and MONARCH? This photograph beautifully demonstrates the variety in the rolling stock collection of the W&L. It also shows that throughout preservation the locomotives based on the line have been well turned out, sporting a wide range of liveries.

*Alan Doig*

CHATTENDEN is another link to the Upnor & Lodge Hill Railway, although it is one of few to remain at the W&L today. It was built in 1949 in Burton-on-Trent by E. E. Baguley and worked on the U&LHR before moving to Broughton Moor in Cumbria and then on to the W&L. It represents the shift underway in the late 1940s, through the 1950s and into the 1960s from steam to diesel on industrial narrow-gauge railways.

*Ron Fisher*

The largest diesel locomotive on the railway is this powerful Diema constructed in Germany for Taiwanese sugar cane work, giving it a curious link to sugar cane steam locomotive JOAN. Brought to the W&L in 2004, it works some of the railway's diesel passenger duties as well as a number of maintenance trains. Here, it ventures onto the road crossing at Cyfronydd.

*Tim Abbott*

This line up of diesels shows CHATTENDEN and the Diema, whose histories have been examined on previous pages, and two further locomotives. The smallest, named FERRET and carrying a pseudo GWR livery, was built by The Hunslet Engine Company for Admiralty work in Wiltshire and the larger, SCOOBY, is of the same type, albeit substantially rebuilt.

*Joe Gunby*

Although not likely to sting, the Wasp is a nimble machine for moving track volunteers between worksites. It was brought to the W&L in 2008 as a regauged Baguley-Drewry trolley built for military use in 1976 at Longtown in Cumbria.

*Andrew Simmonds*

Nicely rounding off this section on resident locomotives is this view of THE COUNTESS and THE EARL in the workshops of the railway at Llanfair.

*Tim Abbott*

Mention NUTTY at the W&L and strong memories of a squat cab are brought back to many. Built not far away at the Sentinel steam wagon works in Shrewsbury for the London Brick Company in 1929, it came to the W&L on loan and was regauged for this purpose from its original 2' 11''. This image shows it approaching the B4385 road crossing at Dolarddyn Road. It is now displayed at the Leighton Buzzard Railway in Bedfordshire.

*W&L Archives*

ORION, or the No. 5 of the Jokioinen Railway in Finland, is a former locomotive of the Welshpool & Llanfair. It worked on its home railway between 1948 and 1964 before heading to the UK; eventually ending up at the W&L in 1983. Powerful and tall in stature, the locomotive did work at the W&L for six years from 2000 before returning to its original home in Finland in 2006.

*Andrew Simmonds*

In 2006, the W&L purchased No. 764.425, a Resita-built locomotive which operated on the line for several years but ultimately proved unsuitable for service in Mid Wales and departed with its sister locomotive No. 764.423, unrestored at the W&L, for Austria in 2016.

*Andrew Simmonds*

Built in 1915, during the First World War, CHEVALLIER hardly looks like the typical Manning Wardle locomotive. This 0-6-2 tank engine was originally based on the Lodge Hill and Upnor Railway, source of many earlier pieces of W&L rolling stock, before moving to the Bowater Paper Mill, home of the modern Sittingbourne and Kemsley Light Railway. In preservation, CHEVALLIER has been principally based on the line at Whipsnade Zoo, from where it was visiting in this 1991 gala photo at Llanfair. It has subsequently visited the line again under new ownership.

*Andrew Simmonds*

SIAM was built in Germany in 1956 by Henschel & Sohn for the Chonburi Sugar Refinery in distant Thailand along with three sisters. Stood at Llanfair, SIAM is captured here at the 1995 gala when visiting the line.

*Andrew Simmonds*

The Sittingbourne and Kemsley Light Railway is one of only three 2' 6'' gauge heritage railways in the UK ensuring a close relationship between them and the W&L. In 2018, their Bagnall locomotive SUPERB visited the W&L and is seen here with JOAN, an earlier derivative of SUPERB's design.

*Andrew Simmonds*

In 2015, the W&L played host to PAKIS BARU No. 5, visiting from the Statfold Barn Railway. This Mallet type of locomotive was built in 1905 for work in Indonesia by Orenstein & Koppel in Germany. During its visit, the No. 5 operated shuttles between Llanfair and Cyfronydd and was the first bogie steam locomotive to operate on the W&L since MONARCH's last runs in 1979.

*Tim Abbott*

Because of the rarity of the W&L's gauge in Britain, visiting locomotives are relatively few by comparison to other railways. Looking for additional motive power for a two year hire, beginning in autumn 2019, the W&L's management turned to the Zillertalbahn in Austria. Resultant negotiations saw No. 2 ZILLERTAL hired to the W&L fresh from overhaul. This sizeable machine predates the 1902-built THE EARL and THE COUNTESS by two years. As home to several Zillertalbahn carriages, the W&L will give visitors to Mid Wales a thoroughly Austrian experience during her time on the line.

*Andrew Simmonds*

UPNOR CASTLE, named in honour of the Elizabethan fort in the town which it formerly operated in, was only a resident of the W&L for a short time. It is seen here in July 1963, shortly after the reopening of the line that year.

*Ron Fisher*

The introduction of passenger services on the W&L when it opened in 1903 was done using three R. Y. Pickering carriages from Wishaw, near Glasgow. These vehicles, which were intricately lined and incorporated stunning wood panel interiors, were sparingly used by passengers aside from market days, when they are reported to have been crammed. The GWR introduced bus services to the communities on the line in the late 1920s and In 1931 passenger trains were withdrawn. The original vehicles were scrapped but, in the early 2000s, replicas were constructed using legacies and donations at the Ffestiniog Railway works at Boston Lodge.

*Andrew Simmonds*

Without tourist traffic in mind, it is unsurprising that the original builders of the Upnor & Lodge Hill Railway carriages did not design vehicles to suit this clientele. The W&L rebuilt two with windows and doors, as demonstrated by this photograph.

*W&L Archive*

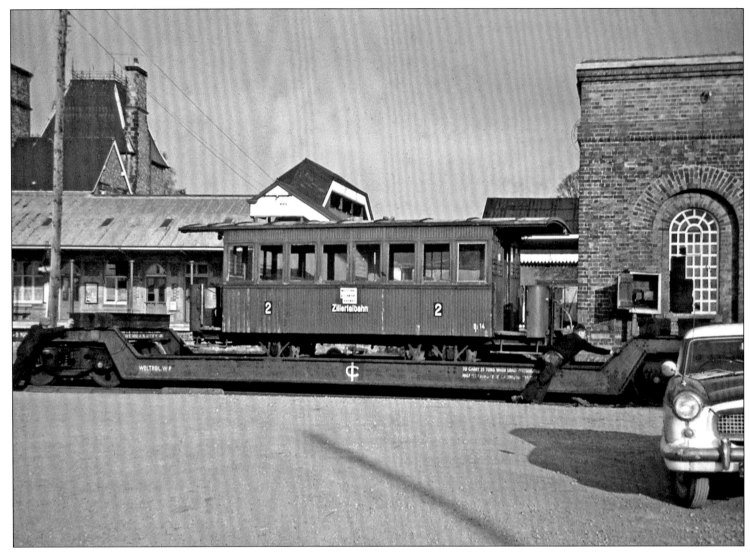

Having found the original Upnor carriages, even after rebuilding, to be less than ideal and with a desire to continue rebuilding the railway beyond Castle Caereinion, the W&L looked abroad for additional carriages. These took the form of Zillertalbahn four-wheelers with vacuum brakes and balcony ends, which were kindly donated to the eager preservationists. Here, B14 can be seen on a British Rail well wagon, bound for the W&L in 1968.

*W&L Archives*

The links of the W&L with Austria have been strengthened further over time with the arrival of further carriages. The second type of Austrian carriage at the W&L are referred to as 'balloons', because of their size and curved nature. This one, finished in the livery of the Salzkammergut Lokalbahn in the railway's own workshops, is a prime example.

*Tim Abbott*

As well as acquiring No. 85 upon the closure of the Sierra Leone rail network, the W&L took the opportunity to bolster its carriage fleet with four 'Independence' carriages, named as such because of their gifting by the UK government when Sierra Leone gained independence in 1961. Here, No.1040 is unloaded at Castle Caereinion.

*Bruce Webber*

As the W&L has continued to grow, the Independence carriages of the SLR have been used less, though their presence in the 1980s and 1990s as everyday vehicles is strong in images of the period. Eventually, one was sold on to the South Tynedale Railway where it is now a buffet car and one was dismantled for spares while the other two were restored in Romania. Here, one of the vehicles returns.

*Triston Lister*

Recently, the W&L has been able to fund the rebuilding of two Hungarian MÁV carriages to better accommodate less-able visitors thanks to the Department of Transport and Rail Standard and Safety Board's Challenge Fund. This work was carried out at Barrow Hill in Derbyshire and these carriages are now a staple of the majority of W&L trains.

*Ron Fisher*

A number of original W&L wagons survive into preservation allowing for the operation of demonstration goods trains and helping the railway to meet its educational aim.

*Andrew Simmonds*

Preservation has to incorporate a good helping of fun to keep volunteer morale up. During the 1960s and early 1970s, a chief source of amusement for volunteers was to emulate British Rail's Motorail service using a flat wagon.

*W&L Archives*

The visit of *Blue Peter* in 1969 evidently caused quite the local stir! Local school children were carried on a special train between Llanfair and Castle Caereinion, allowing for ample shots for the TV crews. On the return journey, however, THE EARL ran short of water and had to be taken for refilling.

*John Bancroft*

HRH Prince Charles came to the railway in 2002, driving THE COUNTESS as well as meeting volunteers. The author feels confident that His Royal Highness enjoyed his visit.
*David Marsh*

After the end of its boiler ticket in 2010, No. 85 spent a period on display at Locomotion, the National Railway Museum at Shildon. For its return journey to the W&L in 2017, a scheme was devised which saw the locomotive enjoy a 'Grand Tour' of museums around the UK including Blist Hill Victorian Village in Ironbridge and Hull Streetlife Museum. This image shows it at the London Museum of Water and Steam at Kew, with the Sierra Leone High Commissioner sharing his memories of his nation's former railway network.

*Tim Abbott*

Multiple class survivors are relatively rare in narrow gauge preservation when compared to standard gauge counterparts. The Sierra Leone National Railway Museum is home to No. 81, the sister engine of No. 85. It shares the museum with several large diesel locomotives, an impressive Beyer Garratt and a dainty Manning Wardle named NELLIE.

*William Bickers Jones*

The W&L, like all other heritage railways, has to run an extensive events programme to fundraise to cover fixed costs and restorations. One such event is the Santa Specials, run in the traditional style with Father Christmas on-board handing out presents. This photograph from 2017 shows a suitably snowy scene, though weather conditions prevailed against many visitors and, as a result, one train during this weekend carried only one family!

*Kevin Heywood*

DOUGAL, while not large enough to haul regular trains, has performed at events such as the Shrewsbury Steam Rally. Perhaps beyond anyone's imagination, it has also spent several months in Taiwan! Sent to represent the W&L at a twinning event, it ran at several of the Taiwan Sugar Company's events, this company operating five heritage lines in Taiwan in 2018.

*Andrew Charman*

Gala events are particularly popular at the W&L. This is likely a result of the wide range of locomotives and rolling stock that can be used to make up a myriad of different trains, plus the Garden Railway Exhibition held in the adjacent school. This image shows THE EARL departing Llanfair with a vintage train of replica Pickering carriages in 2015.

*Geoff Gauntlett*

Country Railway weekends are a former feature of the railway's calendar, highlighting the agricultural heritage of the communities the W&L operates through. In 2005, The Earl stands on a goods train with a farmer's lorry.

*David Marsh*

Because the W&L is able to replicate the two periods of Great Western and British Railways operation so effectively, the line has become a hotspot for photo charters. This image shows THE EARL, deliberately weathered, on a short goods train heading up the Golfa bank. Forming the first section from Welshpool and beginning as soon as trains leave Welshpool, the Golfa, with its twisting route and wooded nature, makes for an amazing experience.

*Lewis Day*

Having tackled the Golfa bank and passed through the first halt, Sylfaen, THE EARL now drifts lazily towards Llanfair, perhaps with some wagons to drop off or collect on route. In reality, this day was THE EARL's last in steam before a thorough overhaul at the Vale of Rheidol Railway.

*Lewis Day*

The W&L continues to operate past a number of operational farms today, all contributing to the success of the local economy and adding to the 'sights to see' from W&L trains. JOAN is seen here leading a rare train of all-brown liveried Austrian carriages.

*Steve Sedgwick*

JOAN, the West Indies Kerr Stuart, is seen here on a short goods trains during the 2018 President's Day event.

*Tom White*

With no sign of modern life and a handful of wagons in tow, THE EARL heads towards Cyfronydd on a photographic charter.

*Lewis Day*

This 2013 gala recreation of the Stephenson Locomotive Society special on the last train on the 3rd November 1956 is seen on the approach to Llanfair, passing the now out of use water tower on this stretch. THE EARL is not taxed here in comparison to the original special which was crowded and featured several more open wagons.

*Tim Abbott*

The W&L station building at Welshpool could have been stood there for the last 100 years by the judgement of sight alone. In reality, it is a much more recent addition being the refurbished station building from Eardisley on the Hereford, Hay & Brecon Railway and is a demonstration to heritage railways everywhere of how to provide good visitor facilities while not compromising the appearance of a station.

*Andrew Simmonds*

Developed over time, Llanfair Caereinion (to give it its full name) is a terminus bustling on a 2018 gala day in this scene. This station is the main hub of the railway, with offices and workshops as well as visitor amenities such as tearoom, shop and Llanfair Connections, the W&L's visitor centre.

*Tim Abbott*

It is only apt to mark the dedication of volunteers, members and the community in the preservation of their railway in this book. The W&L could simply not survive without men and women, committed to the renewal and development of our line, battling adversity for the benefit of us all. To them we say, thank you. (In this image, THE EARL is deliberately dirtied for a photo charter, and is not regularly turned out in this state!)

*Lewis Day*

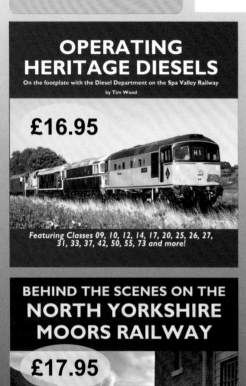
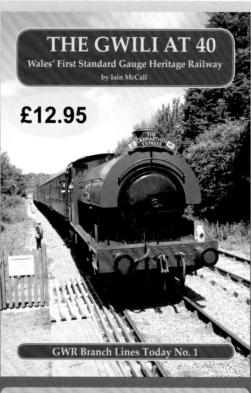